Molecular Cathedral
The Poetry of John Lent

Molecular Cathedral
The Poetry of John Lent

Selected
with an
introduction by
Jake Kennedy
and an
afterword by
John Lent

LAURIER POETRY SERIES

WILFRID LAURIER
UNIVERSITY PRESS

Wilfrid Laurier University Press acknowledges the support of the Canada Council for the Arts for our publishing program. We acknowledge the financial support of the Government of Canada through the Canada Book Fund for our publishing activities. Funding provided by the Government of Ontario and the Ontario Arts Council. This work was supported by the Research Support Fund.

Library and Archives Canada Cataloguing in Publication

Title: Molecular cathedral : the poetry of John Lent / selected with an introduction by
    Jake Kennedy and an afterword by John Lent.
Other titles: Molecular cathedral (Compilation)
Names: Lent, John, author. | Kennedy, Jake, 1972– editor.
Series: Laurier poetry series.
Description: Series statement: Laurier poetry series | Includes bibliographical references.
Identifiers: Canadiana (print) 20240297725 | Canadiana (ebook) 20240297733 |
    ISBN 9781771126373 (softcover) | ISBN 9781771126397 (PDF) | ISBN 9781771126380 (EPUB)
Subjects: LCGFT: Poetry.
Classification: LCC PS8573.E58 M54 2024 | DDC C811/.54—dc23

Front cover image: detail from *Say Yes* (2023) by Jude Clarke, 29" x 37", mixed media, conté, watercolour, and soft pastel. Reproduced with kind permission of the artist.
Series design by P.J. Woodland.
Cover layout by Blakeley and Blakeley.
Interior layout by Mike Bechthold.

This book is printed on FSC® certified paper. It contains recycled materials and other controlled sources, is processed chlorine free, and is manufactured using biogas energy.

Printed in Canada

Wilfrid Laurier University Press is located on the Haldimand Tract, part of the traditional territories of the Haudenosaunee, Anishnaabe, and Neutral Peoples. This land is part of the Dish with One Spoon Treaty between the Haudenosaunee and Anishnaabe Peoples and symbolizes the agreement to share, to protect our resources, and not to engage in conflict. We are grateful to the Indigenous Peoples who continue to care for and remain interconnected with this land. Through the work we publish in partnership with our authors, we seek to honour our local and larger community relationships, and to engage with the diversity of collective knowledge integral to responsible scholarly and cultural exchange.

For my brothers and sisters, Susan Lent, Harry Lent,
Frank Lent, Mary Lou Lee, Michael Lent, and Tim Lent

Table of Contents

Foreword

I am happy to serve as the general editor for the Laurier Poetry Series, the development and growth of which I have followed from its early days. My gratitude goes to Neil Besner and Brian Henderson, who conceived of the Laurier Poetry Series in 2002 as a way to offer a more robust selection of a single poet's work than could be found in an anthology. In 2004, the Laurier Poetry Series launched the first volume, Catherine Hunter's selection of the poems of Lorna Crozier, *Before the First Word*. Neil served as General Editor for all volumes until he was joined in 2016 by Brian, when he left his role as WLU Press's Director. In an act of commitment to poetry publication that is nothing short of inspiring, the Laurier Poetry Series expanded to a list of thirty-three fascinating titles under their leadership.

The retirement of the original editors in 2019 gave me a surprising historical jolt. But thinking historically is a good way to revisit the original plans for the series, and to think towards the future. Under my editorial eye, the series will retain its original aim to produce volumes of poetry made widely available to new readers, including undergraduate students at universities or colleges, and to a general readership who wish for "more poetry in their poetry." WLU Press also retains its commitment to produce beautiful volumes and to alert readers to poems that remain vital to thinking about urgencies of the contemporary moment. It is a reality that poetry books are produced in smaller print runs and often on a shoestring, and as a consequence, original collections of poetry tend to go out of print too quickly and far too precipitously. The series has the added goal of bringing poems from out-of-print collections back into the public eye and the public discourse. The Press's commitment to the work of literary studies includes choosing editors for each volume who can reflect deeply on the body of work, as well as inviting original after-essays from the poets themselves.

As we embark on this next turn of the series, access is our watchword. Canadian literature has undeniably had a checkered history of exclusionary practices, so who gets the nod and who takes part in discussions—as readers and as writers—of Canadian poetry? In the classroom, it is my privilege and my task to introduce a generation of students to the practice of reading poetry as a vital thread in cultural, social, and political conversations, conversations that challenge ideas about Canada and seek to illuminate and bring to consciousness better futures. For that work, I want access to as many voices on the page, and as robust a selection of poems from those voices, as I can get my hands on. This is the language of the bibliophile, the craver of books, the person whose pedagogical pleasure comes from putting poetry books into the hands of others and saying, simply, "Read this, and we'll talk." Multi-author anthologies do not always usefully demonstrate to readers how a poet's work shifts and changes over the years, nor do they always display the ways that a single poet's poems speak to and with and sometimes usefully against one another. I want at my elbow, in every discussion, inside and outside the classroom, our best poetic practitioners. I want books that offer not just a few poems, but dozens: selected volumes not only by the splashiest prize winners but also significantly by poets who have been lifting and carrying a full cultural backpack for decades. To quote Neil Besner, who wrote in his 2016 General Editor's introduction, "What a tremendous wealth of poets and reader we have here! What vital riches!" I couldn't agree more and am grateful for the chance to bring these poets to you, or bring them back to you.

—*Tanis MacDonald*
General Editor

Biographical Note

John Lent was born in 1948 in Antigonish, Nova Scotia, but has lived for the last forty-five years in the Okanagan (Syilx territory), mostly in the city of Vernon, British Columbia. John taught English literature and creative writing at Okanagan College for over thirty years and helped establish the Kalamalka New Writers' Society, the Kalamalka Institute for Working Writers, and the Kalamalka Press before retiring from the College in 2011. John is a novelist, short-story writer, poet, and singer/songwriter. His first poetry book, *A Rock Solid*, was published in 1978 by Dreadnaught Press. John is the author of eight books of poetry and his most recent collection is *A Matins Flywheel* (Thistledown, 2019). He has been a Writer-in-Residence at Red Deer College as well as a visiting writer at the Banff Centre for the Arts, the Wallace Stegner House, the Sage Hill Writing Experience, and the Victoria School of Writing. John is currently working on a new experimental poetry/memoir manuscript entitled *There She Is*. When not writing, John is usually out walking with his beloved wife, painter Jude Clarke, and their Welsh springer spaniel, the irrepressible and one-of-a-kind Mosey.

Introduction
At the Junction of the Eye and Heart

This book is entitled *Molecular Cathedral* but here are some other titles that were vying for attention: *Gift of Blood, Some Sensual Bread, Discovered Confluences, Handel and the Band, Hybrid, After Midnight, Ambiguous Vacuums, Could Be Endless, Tricky Grid Home, To Crack the Night, Voices Freed from Stone, Goin' Down the Road, Sharing Lifting Planes, Field of Vision, More Coffee for the Long Ride Back, After All the Bullshit the Peace of Gardens, God's in the Toaster, Weightless, The Real Soil, It Is and Deserves, Mystery and Quotidia, Covenant with Perspective, Holy Mathematics, 99th Street in the Rain, All For Jude ...*

I hope these also-rans point out the wildness, richness, dynamism, constancies, and even gorgeous contradictions—not to mention the luminous reach—of John Lent's forty-five-year body of work in poetry. Kind reader, I need to tell you that Lent is that most extraordinary thing: an utterly ardent artist who—despite all of the darknesses and struggles he documents—remains committed to seeking what is true and liberatory and beautiful. So, welcome in, eh? And before we follow the trajectory of Lent's seven core books of poetry, I wonder if I could, right away, just tell you a few stories about the man? I'd love for you to have a fuller sense of both his humanity and his commitment to making.

In the early '90s, I was studying writing at York University with the two Dons: Coles and Summerhayes. These teacher-poets—while both brilliant and unforgettable—were worlds apart from each other in a number of ways. Coles was lean and sophisticated and elegant and generally interested in the serious. Summerhayes was bearish and self-deprecating and earthy and generally interested in whatever might upend the serious. As far as I can tell, the only thing the two Dons agreed on was that John Lent was a very good man and a very good poet. So my introduction to Lent's work and character arrived via endorsements from these two entirely opposed artists. What was immediately intriguing for me was to wonder how any one poet-person might harmonize such disparate poetics and personalities. And all of the abundant (to use a Lent word) answers would be there for me, of course, in Lent's resplendent work.

What I found in Lent was the erudition of Coles, for sure. But I also saw the of-this-real-earth and of-this-real-time-ness of Summerhayes, too. In Lent's work, there are references to literary theorists, artists, poets, philosophers, and historians and—at the same time—you'll see how regularly he *names* his subjects and captures them so richly, sometimes hilariously, always movingly, in their dailiness. Lent is indeed a kind of marriage of the Dons but he is also something quite beyond these poets, too. Specifically, Lent's work mines and is preoccupied with both the magic and the ordinariness of consciousness. It's as if, in Lent's poems, every flickering of the brain's energy is tracked and transformed into—or is revealed to us as—art.

When I first got to meet Lent, in around 2006, it was after I was lucky enough to secure a teaching position at Okanagan College (Syilx territory). By this point, I was quite familiar with his poetry but I wasn't aware fully—being a typical Toronto-centric Ontarian—of his legendary reputation as a teacher and mentor throughout the Okanagan Valley and indeed throughout the entire west coast. But since I had the pleasure of working alongside Lent for several years in the English department before his retirement in 2011, I got to see, first-hand, his humility and his wisdom, his generosity and his abiding joy, his convictions and his dedications. Here's one small example of Lent's standing and popularity in our community. Shortly after I was hired, we had an English department meeting in the early fall and then some of us (including Lent) went to a coffee shop afterwards in Kelowna. I wanted rather desperately to talk poetry with Lent but it was impossible because—in my recollection—six people (some former students, some writers, some friends, and some all three) recognized him and stopped by the table to catch up and laugh. And this is the way it would continue to be going forward, whether on campus or at a reading or at a conference; admirers would gather around Lent. That's when I first realized that he was, in a way, a rock star with a deep sense of humility.

Since Lent's retirement, I've had the unique delight to spend time with and interview this ever-searching, ever-inspired poet. Lent has become a close friend but he is also and always to me and, I know, to so many others, the writer who shows the way for us. I propose that you can read every one of his books as a conscientious and ongoing experiment in hybrid forms. Lent shows the way in terms of innovative aesthetics, and he also guides us in terms of right conduct and kindness in the trade. For instance, Lent has visited my creative writing classrooms approximately twenty times and there is never any ego or posturing. What Lent does, I've noticed, is *listen* to the students and ask serious, engaged questions. He doesn't declaim and he doesn't hit writerly poses—he instead offers up the world of art as wondrously available to everyone in the room. What results after every Lent visit is simply abiding evidence of how he empowers emerging writers—how he reminds them of their importance and of the value of their own visions and of their own landscapes.

The only other thing I'd like to add, before we move into a consideration of Lent's poems, is how "humanness" or so-called "niceness" is so maddeningly underappreciated as a quality of an artist. I would venture that Lent is not so much a "nice guy" as he is an artist of deep compassion. What such deep compassion reveals to me is necessarily a correspondingly profound awareness of darkness and suffering. I don't think anyone can feel for the other, reach out to the other, without an abiding and lived sense of how far apart and lost we usually are from our fellow beings. Lent, in a way, is *not nice at all* if nice merely means naïve or pleasant; he is rather—and so much more pyrotechnically—in touch with the wonders and fathoms of the heart. That's why, I contend, that Lent is so present, so understanding, and so vital in his interactions and in his extraordinary body of work.

* * *

Lent's first book of poems, *A Rock Solid*, appeared in 1978, in a limited edition with a striking design by Toronto's Dreadnaught Press. The poem is a sequence that plays out over nine separate cards that are themselves contained within a four-panel cardstock fold, slipped inside a stylish sleeve. The book opens with an "an attempted prelude," as Lent writes, printed on the inside of the main four-panel card. And this prelude, he continues, is like "the wash you have to use first if you're working in watercolour." Here Lent applies a technique of visual art to explain the subtle qualities of his literary text. Lent has a background in painting, and his devoted partner, Jude Clarke, is also an established artist, and so these cross-disciplinary analogies are, I think, rather organic for him. (We will see later, too, how crucial music is to Lent's understanding of literary form and improvisation.) Lent teaches us how to transform, so to speak, form itself—a book need not only be read with literary "logic." It may also be understood as painterly or architectural or sonic or sculptural.

What's most interesting about the "attempted prelude" is how it introduces the reader to one "who is a compulsive consumptive" and "who laughs a lot" and "who abstracts a moment instead of contracting it" and "who sits in the house a lot, listens to CBC too much, and thinks." This Lent-like persona is always ruminating and is—as you may already infer from these few quotations—always dependably, charmingly honest, and uninflated. By the conclusion of the prelude, the reader is introduced to an intensely thoughtful subject: a persona who is always wondering about the intersection of the abstract moment (the wandering thought regarding, say, "the simple power to appreciate") and the concrete moment (this "grunting sack of blood and bone" right here): how to blend, apprehend, and know them both.

Most of Lent's abiding themes are vividly present in this early work: abstract vs. concrete; thinking vs. doing; desire vs. contentment; the mind vs. the body; family vs. solitude; class vs. aspiration; addiction vs. control; love vs. art. Of course, in Lent's work, these themes are not ultimately binaries so much as they are generative intermixings. In the same way, I think, that Lent intertwines poetry and prose in his unruly forms he also reveals the braid of his enduring themes.

While the sharp-eared reader might notice a somewhat more pronounced reliance on repetition in this first book than in later Lent works, as well as denser language and references (the word "Qliphoth," for instance), it has a remarkably Lent-distinct sound. Specifically, even in this early text, which Lent wrote in his late twenties, one can hear the poet determined to find—without resorting to any fashionable ironies— clarities: "it's all so exquisite, in any light you choose." Lent's poet-persona is always a sensitive receiver for every gorgeous or disturbing frequency. In all of his work, he is committed to the tuning of such sounds with the final recognition of *static* as constitutive of all transmissions. I think this is one of his most amazing discoveries.

* * *

Wood Lake Music—a sui generis long poem—appeared in 1982 and is another example of Lent employing a hybrid form. The book combines newspaper reports, prose poems, free verse poetry, conversation, documentary. *Wood Lake Music*, as you'll note in these selections, also employs a predominantly third-person perspective so the vantage of the poems often feels similar to something more like a novel or short story experience. A reader feels the spareness of the free verse but also the depth and reach of a narrative in which a "he" is followed up and down the Okanagan Valley. We intuit that the "he" of the text resembles Lent himself, and gain deep access to this persona's thoughts and motivations, but always with the added remove of that narrator-like distance. It's an impressive, paradoxical technique that ensures both autobiographical intimacy and a rich, fictive, bracketed perspective.

As the book blends prose and poetry, it also meditates on race and class and region. The book begins with an opening newspaper report from the *Penticton Herald* which outlines growing tensions between French-Canadian migrant fruit workers and the local Osoyoos (South Okanagan) population. One of the "statics" that Lent is keen to explore here involves the exposure of racial tensions (and of explicit racism) in this tourist-dependent, leisure-driven landscape so determined to forward a "well-tuned" picture of Okanagan life. Woven through these political realities are, of course, the persona's own explorations of "how to think" and "how to be" in light of such evident problems of belonging. I have called *Wood Lake Music* a long poem and it is also a chronicle that tracks thinking as desire. Lent moves through the thinking mind as if it's a luminous diorama—he wants to both honour and document every burst of light:

driving asphalt rising · driving rain falling
between these the shifting lake and its
cowled blinking mountains and him

drawn homeward from his job on a Friday afternoon
he is interpreting everything:

the beginning of the world

Driving is so important in Lent's work particularly as it gains him access to solitude, immediate natural landscapes, and *textures*. That last noun might seem either out of place or too diminutive compared to others in the list, but I hope you'll also see in Lent's world that he boasts a sculptor's or carpenter's understanding for the tactile. Lent is not just "interpreting everything" but also often attempting to reach and handle—right in the midst of the daily world—all of its contours. This is the second of what I think of as Lent's powerful discoveries: to see poetry as captured consciousness. It is stunning to me how he shows the mysterious complexities of the mind—yes, we are in the car driving, but we are also the rain and the shifting lake and the mountains blinking and, indeed, the world itself.

* * *

Lent's fascinating 1984 collection, *Frieze*, establishes its preoccupations with three revealing epigraphs. The first one is from British novelist Lawrence Durrell, the second is from American short story writer William Kotzwinkle, and the third and final quotation is from the anonymous Maritimes' ballad "Goin' Down the Road." The first and last epigraphs confirm the unusual, dynamic intermixing of Lent's aesthetics and inheritances. Durrell's quotation is a lengthy, dense, expansive meditation on landscape and desire; it achieves its effects through accretion and high rhetoric. The final quotation is spare and unpretentious and melancholy: "So I'm goin' down the road, boys / I'm seekin' what I'm owed, boys / And I guess it must get better / If far enough I go." Part of the book's tensions— and, of course, part of the interplay of all of Lent's oeuvre—is here in the elevated and the earthly, in the world of high art *and* on the common roads of folk. This is the third Lentian discovery as I see it: not only should such hierarchies be subverted but the so-called common or "low" and the so-called rarified or "high" should be viewed merely as different facets of the same ongoing wonder of being.

If you look at the poem "Wascana Geese, Lifting," you might also notice one more level to this last-noted discovery. Lent not only never takes himself too seriously but in fact uses a recognition of absurdity as the springboard into revelation. After Lent has his reader imagine these picturesque geese (whom he suspects of being "aware of self-parody"), and after he proposes to invite them to his house to don sunglasses and drink scotch, he concludes the exquisite poem:

> but I suspect my dream of
> half-smiles here   and feathered nods
> that ache for the perfect audience
> is real enough
>
> that want of the sharing lifting planes
> of laughter gathers   invades
> in a communal sweep of wings   rises
> in a buffeting crescendo
> of hollow bones

You can feel the huge fluttering music of their lift-off as if the book itself, all of the pages, are riffling and containing the flock. But what Lent does here without any irony at all is say "hey, I know you've seen such sights before but here's where my mind takes me" and that journey is captivating and splendid and—most significantly—"real enough."

Realness is *enough* because it's always imbued with magic and, necessarily, magic is only magical because it's inseparable from the real. In Lent's 1990 *The Face in the Garden*, these conceptions are extended in dazzling fashion. First of all, the initial half of the book is autobiographical fiction while the second half pivots into poetry proper. While this shift into poetry is signaled most obviously, of course, by the line breaks, the quality and complexity of thinking is merely an extension of the rich, seemingly ceaseless wonderings of the narrator(s)—sometimes in first-person and sometimes in third-person modes. There's a fluency on the level of consciousness that extends across the two forms until a reader doesn't really feel them as distinct but rather as complementary.

The Face in the Garden opens with a revealing epigraph from 17th-century poet Andrew Marvell's "Upon Appleton House." This excerpt speaks of "things greater are in less contained" until we understand that the achievement of "holy mathematics" is aligned with humility. *The Face in the Garden*—page by page—demonstrates this revelation. There is a section in the prose portions of the book in which the narrator worries that he has become a "failed hermit, a timorous recluse." The narrator even imagines himself as a tertiary character in a film being dismissed by viewers in their post-viewing debrief. In Lent's work, there is almost always third-order thinking (or "triple thinking" as John often says in conversation) until the persona is watching himself watch himself be watched. This kind of intense scrutiny and sensitivity with respect to the workings of the mind could result in paralysis but not so in Lent; instead, it's a revelation. Lent maps all of the convolutions of the mind ("I am a living thing obsessed by its life," he writes in "Facing the Gardens") until he's reminded of the sublimity of the daily. The poems honour humility, and in that honouring, find their way towards those holy mathematics.

* * *

There is a beautiful line from Italo Calvino in which he marvels at Franz Kafka's commitment to clarity and the resultant hallucinatory effect: "The true challenge for a writer is to speak of the intricate tangle of our situation using a language so seemingly transparent that it creates a sense of hallucination." What's so powerful here in Calvino's quotation is the interaction of incompatibilities: tangles, hallucinations, transparencies. I think there's a way that Lent's work—though employing a style far different from Kafka's—exemplifies this unaffected, crystalline rightness. In his 2000 collection, *Black Horses, Cobalt Suns*, Lent's technique achieves its perfection of "seemingly transparent language." In this book he is constantly working to get at the true: no posturing, no bardic brashness, no irony. As he notes on the opening page of that collection, his art is ever in the service of a sought-for but always protean beauty: "the shift being the thing itself."

Black Horses, Cobalt Suns also formally declares Lent's ultimately abiding theme—love. In our (long) contemporary moment in which aloofness and the sardonic have dominated literary aesthetics, Lent's commitment to exploring "love" threatens to sound sentimental or overly plain or even naïve. It's not surprising that such terms have often been used historically, say, to disparage feminist or revolutionary poetics generally. Lent's commitment is not to the trend or market but rather to the Calvino-esque, truthful hallucination. He meets the reader at the "junction of the eye and the heart" and is vigilant about any overly easy move towards the cynical or ironic. The love-propelled emphasis of his work—on view in Poem 9, for example—is a move to redemption that is never separable from memory or presence; we are here, Lent reveals, we get to have these bodies and these regrets and these miraculous nows.

* * *

Both *Cantilevered Songs* and *A Matins Flywheel* reveal the mature style and vibrant ideals of Lent's vision. Consider his poem "Taking Jude Out for Breakfast…" in which the speaker recognizes ultimately that "this is enough" and finds a kind of radical insight on and in "the real soil." In this poem and in Lent's work broadly, he's not so much in search of lost time but *in time* completely. He sees the past everywhere in the now and he wonders at the parallels (or criss-crossings) of time—always with a final belief in the miraculousness of the ho-hum minutes and hours. Lent's rocking poem—and the one that lends this collection its title—"Molecular Cathedral" opens with a dense, challenging stanza about coming to terms with solipsism, selfishness, guilt. He explores these themes personally but also as cultural markers. What I note, though, is how operative Lent's seemingly jokey, throw-away sounds are: "There ya go!" and "Holy crap!" These sounds are the sounds of—to my ear at least—real life and they gain access to the miraculous precisely because Lent shows to his readers our manynesses. I'll leave you, as a first-step into the wondrous structures of Lent's body of work, with this marvelous portal:

> this incarnation we are,
> the word made flesh, a molecular cathedral straining
> within itself, its medieval, gothic balances
> and counter-turns and arches and cross-bracing,
> its unimaginable architecture a gift
> that *requires* selfishness as a *pledge* not
> a betrayal of love: the harder
> path even.

—*Jake Kennedy*

Works Cited

Calvino, Italo. "The Written Word and the Unwritten Word." Trans. Ann Goldstein. *Paris Review Daily*. https://www.theparisreview.org/blog/2023/01/05/the-written-world-and-the-unwritten-world/ Accessed January 6, 2023.

Prelude

Read this as an attempted prelude. Like the wash you have to use first if you're working in watercolor. It's a base for the colors, the figures, the worlds which follow.

anyone
who is a compulsive
consumptive. Rising from somewhere, the Maritimes likely, and nurtured in Edmonton, unfolding like a roseate tapeworm in the bowels of impulse, a gift of blood: a membrane separating the tissues of thought and action. Thinking sharp and focused surfaces, control: symmetrical fulfilment and use. Acting a dull and cluttered chaos: asymmetrical descent into formlessness and decay. Delicious.

who is not funny no matter how he is abstracted into explanation, into system.

who consists in the pleasure of a quick eye, a quick grasp: the angle of the light through the fogged window here; the gesture of the day as it opens there; an elusive pattern which coalesces in abstraction: the simple power to appreciate.

who consists in the pleasure of plotted violence; as if his consumptions were a fanning concrete appendage: a flowing cloak of cigarette packages, beer cases, Calona Vermouth bottles, modular units of time spent in one bar or another; a hand on the sweat on a woman's forehead, a hand on his own prick, or something, or anything, to take in, to sense. Some sensual bread to distract that eye, that grasp, that love. Manna of indulgence.

who is a cartoon. And, who is sometimes aware of this.

who is a grunting sack of blood and bone.

who is disappointed often.

who is frightened he might slip into either of these sides completely.

who laughs a lot.

who feels guilty often.

who abstracts a moment instead of contracting it.

who is a compulsive keeper-of-diaries. Has them numbered on a shelf. Is writing in Number Five now. The numbers are marked on masking tape, and the diaries look good when they're lined up side by side. Who, of course, does not make daily entries. Instead, attempts to surround only the charged moments. Could be thinking of Stephen Dedalus at such times. Except. Except.

who has been transformed by two irregular years of ascent and descent in Nelson, BC. Who wants to be honest now.

who is fighting through either wall to real surfaces: objects, faces, smells, plants, gravel, asphalt, wind.

who examines everything.

who wrote once: 'October 3, 1973. I feel so good today. When the concrete surround and the abstract surround discover confluence, that's magic. What a rush! That's how I felt crossing the bridge today, looking at the valley, singing Jesse Winchester's "Payday" as loudly as I could.'

and yet: 'October 11, 1973. What a destitute angel. Nervous, twittering, cigarette-infested ball of anticipation. What, in God's name, am I going to do here? Christ! What about that perception about ego/sex I had a couple of weeks ago? Well, what's necessary is sex of some kind.'

who decided to leave a woman he loves, in 1973, in order 'to get myself together,' and rationalized it by getting a job in BC.

who lives in a small but comfortable house on the lake, at the foot of Elephant Mountain, a half-mile on the North Shore from Nelson. Who discovered a new land. Peter Gzowski, Barbara Frum, and Harry Brown don't know much about it.

who sits in the house a lot, listens to CBC too much, and thinks.

who sometimes rolls down the orchard by the star of the yard-light late at night, full of beer, and laughing into the various silences: the multifoliate stars, trees, and lake.

who sometimes just sits and works. Makes an omelette. Plays with the dog. Reads *Penthouse* or Malcolm Lowry.

who makes desperate long-distance phone calls, and who once had a monthly bill for 250 dollars.

who misses Brunswick Avenue.

who misses his lover.

who can't help surrendering to absence, but who tries not to anyway.

who is a compulsive consumptive, rising full of gases like a balloon, but costumed and angled, and rotating, slowly, and on solid ground, and

who is accepting, and

who is ambiguous with smile.

Panel 5

Once you hit the Manitoba border, when you're travelling west, the cultural zones shift. Bars. Draught beer. I had a good apprenticeship in Edmonton: The Corona, The Riviera, The Saxony, The Kingsway, The Klondiker. In Nelson, now, what else is there to do? I'm sitting here, for example, typing, but I'll head into town for a few later on. You don't necessarily get drunk. And you talk. And your fantasies and dreams and visions conspire with the juke-box, the smiles, the grimaces, the ambiguous emotions. And, of course, the scrupulous attendants. The service is great. How many years, Lotus-eaten? And outside, in the silences, the mountains, the prairie sky, are waiting to be named, waiting for eyes.

Panel 9

There are some odd collections of people in Nelson, and scattered throughout the Slocan and Kaslo valleys. Young people mostly. Have come here with great commitments. So many. Have left California, Vancouver, Oakville. Have bought land, built homes, are having one child after another. It appeals to me sometimes. This chaos. The delicious roll of it. This is an unknown place which change has chosen. Naturally, paranoia is a correspondent for change. There's a lot of paranoia here. On both sides. But the valleys. These rolling, folding walls. It's all so exquisite, in any light you choose.

Poem Ten

TEN: Friday, September 19, 4:00 p.m.

1

he had one of those rare fierce talks with her
about relationships   more seriously this time

"When do you know something for sure?" she asked

"Nobody is ever sure.   Of anything."

admits that's his creed
that he delights in this one absolute:
that there can be none   that he hates
them when they're thrown at him

to be able to decide   to act in spite of that

he celebrates

2

rain and the old wipers whacking
slippery when wet signs and he thinks

of Lee   of this:

There was a time when men could say
my life, my job, my home
and still feel clean.
*The poets spoke of earth and heaven.   There were no symbols.**

driving asphalt rising   driving rain falling
between these the shifting lake and its
cowled   blinking mountains   and him

drawn homeward from his job on a Friday afternoon
he is interpreting everything:

the beginning of the world

---

* Dennis Lee, *Civil Elegies*, 1972.

Poem Fifteen

FIFTEEN: Friday, October 3, 2:30 p.m.

1

coming down this morning the fog had been
unique: ragged   low   clinging to the water

he'd risen out of a thicker version of this in Vernon
had broken as usual into sunlight near the army camp
then dropped back down into it after the lookout

unusual: in and out of it and the sun
all the way down   a frayed woolen tunnel
grey   worn so thin in places you almost saw gold

in that last turn into the four lanes
that arc round the south end of Duck Lake
fog   trees   sun   lake   combined and
he felt he was in some mid-sixties French film
birches flicking by autumnal   water flashing
Jean-Paul Belmondo   looking rather serious
driving through the French countryside to Paris
in a sports car   smoking   thinking of her

it is early dawn   we see him sitting there
just before we cut to Catherine Deneuve waking
up suddenly in her bed   lolling her breasts back
into the silvered sheets in a smiled sigh of him

(he'd prefer Geneviève Bujold)

sure   he thinks   so stupid that we refer
our own passage to that impossible memory
of richer landscapes   grown even richer
in our absence   in magazines and movies
the recreation of Europe: sad pilgrimage
what we see needs no references

we even have whispered ghosts   these
chatter about day to day things to one another
stutter   laughing in the wind rushes like leaves

but that's how we interpret these fogs
why we want them   feel comfortable

it does strange things to a landscape
makes invented detail possible: Platonic

like Vaseline on a voyeur's lens he thinks

2

Iraq is interested in a cease fire
it would be   would be holding territory
in Iran   Iran will have none of this

naturally   everybody's wondering

3

sat up alone last night   listening to Handel
then put on the headphones and *The Last Waltz*
got carried away   totally concealed in that energy
wasn't sure if it was the gin that carried him
backwards into an anarchic confidence and half-smiles

or if it was simply the infectious voice of the music:
Van Morrison singing Tura Lura Lura   improvising
the twentieth century out of that old ballad
charming our restless folk music into its new forms:
electricity   concrete   stucco   asphalt   guns
mutant song for mutants: in the transition

Handel and the Band   an emerging eye
caught between these   aspiring

(an eye blinks over a tune in a field   hand turns peat

behind these   in the predictable feudal mansion
an old order whines to itself   looks out of its boredoms
to listen to that tune and chuckle   pick its nose
perfectly   with grace   with symmetry   so lost
in a condescension at the possible

it does not hear the mob in the hallway
approaching this last door   ascending the bloody

staircase   lusting for tomorrow   wanting

a head to think with   confused)

by gin?   by music?

4

the most loathed non-race on the face of
the earth possibly: north americans

hybrid

Wascana Geese, Lifting

my fanning suspicion
that they are aware of self-parody
endears these birds to me
bumping and scraping
fumbling necks over bulbous feathers
pecking one another and the snow
aping vulnerability   burlesquing naïveté
in quizzical jerks   floundering runs on ice

I want them in my living room at night
thirty of them in sunglasses drinking scotch
chuckling over *Front Page Challenge*
butting cigars   snacking
on chips and dip

company

their sense of humour is part of
a hollow-boned certitude of flight
a covenant with perspective
sly acquaintance with horizon

they accommodate our stares
patronize our burgeoning solicitude
our dreams of down and fur
our stretching arms of popcorn
our posturing envious gravity

all this ridiculous in its way
volumes of evidence dilute the vision
into compound steam

but I suspect my dream of
half-smiles here   and feathered nods
that ache for the perfect audience
is real enough

that want of the sharing lifting planes
of laughter gathers   invades
in a communal sweep of wings   rises
in a buffeting crescendo
of hollow bones

Triptych: Seeds

> Perspective was then no longer based on rules of geometry,
> but was achieved, from foreground to horizon, by the
> gradation of tints and tones, suggesting space and volume.
> — Maurice Sérullaz, *Impressionist Painters*

it's over once again
the instant my hand stretches for the briefcase
the elliptical blackboard expands into
intersecting volumes
the field of vision here abstracts itself into
there objects turning

three bodies arch
converge

1.
He doesn't stride into the room
more of a sustained lean forward
etched and original in muscle departures
variations on a theme of nerves
deposit   his grin over the desk
a chuckle launches arms to the brush and the blackboard
the sportcoat tails herringbone the wall
his voice walls the room:

"How many of you guys
have not read *Lycidas*?"

the authority in his voice plays the faces before him
orchestrates a fugue of plotted query and innocence
it is absolute and gentle
like a father's anger overheard in the basement

you have lost his hammer apparently

the sounds of indirect love
interpreted around   beneath
behind this montage of armies marching

no answer from the troops

"Fine."

"This is a poem about the emotion of loss."

"How many of you guys
have had a close relative
or a friend die?"

to a plot of roses

my father stands to face us squarely
his arms reach for the desk's edges
a triangle of nerves releases its gift

between a stare   through this garden   his eyelids blink
the rhetoric of muscles pausing

"This is an elegy."

no romance here
his eyes reach the whole room
touch things

something is exacted
something is lost in this
something feeds

"A pastoral elegy."

his body turns
the hand clasps
the chalk

2.
I've read most of the obituaries
there were quite a few
the School Board donated *The Encyclopaedia Britannica*
to his school   after he died

other things too
stories my father told me
those I overheard my father tell

photographs   one of him young   one old
in my parents' bedroom on the dresser
next to their wedding portrait
beneath my father's degree

not much to go on really

we went back to Nova Scotia that last time though
all eight of us to visit them
I was eleven   he was retired
he sat as the center in a high-ceilinged kitchen
built years ago for the children and Catherine
sat like a fixture in the rocking chair
knifed the air beside the wood stove in semi-circles
flexing his knees

he didn't talk very much

I hardly remember him talking at all
(except at night when I could hear him sometimes
vague   through the floorboards
sometimes clear   though the air-vent)
during the day he simply managed that chair
allowed Catherine to weave and re-weave
bubbles of anecdotes around him
he would nod   break into laughter
chuckle   clean his glasses
stuff his pipe   rearrange his tartan vest
his slippers

on the morning we were leaving
his eyes broke their ritual and seared mine
he leapt up   trance-like
seized me through ambiguities of selves
of years   of possibilities
(it seems that way now)
"I'm never going to see you again.
You be a good boy."

held me in an indirect bristled hug
something to be interpreted

a year later
on the day after we found out
I spent most of my time in the basement
manufacturing grief   trying so hard
conjuring collapse into tears
out of TV shows   movies
so I looked at his photograph
and painted a portrait
"It looks just like him."
my father who couldn't fly down for the funeral
all grief rising at that

I see this man now
standing in the corner of a panelled room
behind a desk   *F.I. Lent, Principal*
the charcoal two-piece suit
that tartan vest
hands in the pant pockets

he is staring out the window
he is thinking about something
his thinning hair   his creased and
folding face   the pipe
the spectacles   the lines behind the rims
around his eyes

these volumes turn to an opening door
"What is it, Harry?"

my father's freckled hand
flat against the mahogany

3.

the job itself is nothing
as vulnerable as those before it
a ten-month contract this time   the chance of renewal
you don't believe you're actually holding it down

you simply catch yourself doing that
surprised by earnestness

Edmonton   Toronto   Nelson   Toronto
Regina now

but the act is everything
after the anxiety   the leaps to organize
the voice always fulfills

something happens to the cynicism too
some thing falls away each time
confronts me like a loss
a perfectly concealed will   forgetting me
so arbitrarily out of time
I'm afraid of a day when that will
allows the voice self-sufficiency
abstraction

you fear a time of visitors arriving
Sunday afternoons possibly   and you laugh
approximately

I live out the flesh as usual   other volumes
and the voice has its way too
I turn to the blackboard
chalk in hand and a smile

"We all know what this is about.
I want to know how it was made."

flip the chalk in my hand
mistake it for the cigarette in the other
laughter

"What choices did he make
from all the possibilities in time
to write this   to put this together?"

my eyebrows rise
face stretches into a sigh
one hand ferrets a pocket

self-deprecating authority
sets it stage

"How would *you* choose from the past
to build *your* life into a portrait?"

one hand reaches for the cigarette package
my eyelids blink
I stare

if some self's child
were watching?

if some self's child
were watching the seed leaving?

if some self's child
were the seed leaving?

Open Line

I wish I were one of those guys sometimes
keep thinking about them   trying to place them

see my mother hoisting the ironing board to one in '52
turning up the radio before descending the stairs to
the wringer-washer   seeping concrete   peeling insulation
or sitting in the kitchen with her tea and the window
a break in her multiplying pregnant routine

but always to his voice

I forget the products it flogged so much then
doesn't matter much   Paulin's Crackers
Surf   Quik   Fab   Kraft Dinner
are my memories   not necessarily her facts
but in and around the voice   these
or something like them close in on her
backdrop to the insinuating smile itself

one greyed morning in Edmonton in the fall of '53
the backyard a warm and checkered balloon of games
my brother and I turn a blistered faulty ladder
into an airplane   straddling its cross-braces
like pilots   thinking clouds and distance
she appears out of the voice to get a picture of this
is she thinking of one of his contests?

driving Regina's Wascana Parkway through hoarfrost now
my whole world here encased in silver this morning
or each part in it shattering in flat white silks
every accumulating detail grown big with whites
assuming the uniform glory we see as children
when the surfaces of things seem the things themselves
when the landscape is sure to the eye and the heart

driving to work to this disc-jockey's open line
like that hoarfrost he is simplifying our world:
he knows everything   and   he knows everybody
he answers each question swiftly plays with

these women   his callers so hesitant at first
but always fascinated eventually   like a child
respecting and loving a drunken parent's dance on payday
they listen to his random abuse   his selective flattery
and he becomes some local anaesthetic   he thinks
some magus conjuring smiles and laughs out of the dry
vacuums sifting   irons slapping cotton   he
oversees ritual phone calls   orchestrates hands
holding coffee mugs   flicking ashes
all this   quite naturally   my fantasy
my screenplay of his influence   his power

and yet   before I turn the key off in the parking lot
I want all my misplaced emotions to jam the channels
to intervene for once: I have always loved you
soft woman   folding futures so naturally
in the midst of all this noise
folding me into you open lines so gently
in spite of all his static

you tolerate him   are even entertained
by his continuous bumptious force
you endure his indulgences for the rest of us
allow him to reduce the world   but you
admit him into your private dancing too

think of my mother's own closed circles then
beneath my childish photograph of her silvered silks
the moment after she snaps the camera and turns
into our house again   and his voice

I wish I were one of those guys sometimes
could be anonymous   could hear her voice
dancing: *he is outside in the backyard*
is learning to fly he thinks

excerpt from Frieze

this job seems less than ordinary
invisible   some people think that of
teaching   think of its cancer: how that
circles the brain like   fever   how that
prevents heart in songs

some people fear my job

for their own reasons

I've grown used to being invisible
soundless   in all this noise
if I were to raise my voice with
theirs   to sing my songs   somehow
song would fall headlong   into
the facts of my job   stone
dropped from a trestled bridge
is lost to the flashing   reflection
above it   then voice is carried
tumbling   acquires fresh silts
a more quiet home against that clear
violent   rush

so you have to scream some songs   too
bad   or they turn to stone   silence

now   I have voices to free from stone
must grown violent in chords   shout

Enclosed Garden, 1

have been tending private gardens instead

pass through the grey film of the door
descend blue stairs armed with clippers
trowels   gloves   pails   rakes   a variety of
sprinklers on hoses   the lawnmower

groom lawns and flower beds
plant annuals   a clematis
a Virginia creeper

ceremoniously install a tamarisk
a sun-burst locust

trying to break the linear mathematics
of our standard city lot

and yet simultaneously
I attempt to manicure this garden
into another order

we commit this contradiction on ourselves
not as innocent as instinct versus reason

as if contrary selves
perceived alternate beauties
we are at war
growing ourselves chaotically
rearranging   reordering

this garden

is always two photographs of itself
one superimposed upon another

they never match up

these photos

unless a third synthetic self
leans back into this striped canvas chair
stretches its limbs

at peace in this vortex of wills

watches the water whirl round and round

drenching a porous ground with

possibility

The Unnecessary Torture of Summer Nights

the street is a caragana of quiets tonight
so thick so loud you'd think something in it
would crack and shred these hesitations of
light and wind   these pauses in air

but the street sighs into its own shadows and sleeps
its different dreams

I sit in the outset of these territories
barely breathing on the porch step: a conscious eye
in the heart of this unconsciousness
a scythe through wheat

my dog wedges herself closer to me
for protection

(and we have invented the usual
signs to define ourselves in this
then judge ourselves accordingly
finally despair of the signs
why would we be enclosed by them?

and we have scripted the usual
films of our day to day lives in this
cast ourselves in a variety of roles
then abhor the movie and its heroes
why would we want to watch ourselves
watching ourselves like this?

"It's all in the mind."

that's where it is all right

why would we want to suffer
these distances by such callous
measurements?)

streetlamps pace and orchestrate the dark
trail their auras down the misting street

to the corner where the penny-candy store's
Coca-Cola sign strokes the highway
like something sure

beneath these dark panels
the cracked sidewalks sift off into abstraction
evanesce into charcoal

living room windows cast fuses of light
like the glowing tubers of circus tents
over the stretched geography of lawns
while one unattended sprinkler cuts
through the quiet a lion-tamer's whip
whirling circles

my feet fumble unconsciously for leverage
rearrange their gravity on the wooden steps
as my dog attempts even closer contact
nudging her encrusted bum onto my pantleg

over my shoes to the south
the looming black silhouettes of a maple and elm
the moon a grail in gnarled fingers
those intricate histories

there is nothing to say

I sit in this garden
the air a fuse in my face
the light and heat of summer
abstracted by night

what would I want to say anyway?

(would it be better
if the trucks rolled in
cameras hoisted down onto dollies
the crew instructed
the director poised
in certitudes?

could I film a better version of this?
me the solitary wise vortex of the scene
designed to make the frantic suffer
toss in sleep for parallel perfections
excluded from this one?

isn't it enough?
a man sits before the oncoming summer rain
sifts in these silences
for the silences themselves?

is here in this blast of living
an eye on the imperfections of Eden?

must we always diminish ourselves
package our going in order to see it

disappoint ourselves in mirrors?)

rain descends like rain
drapes this naked world in sighs

I cannot believe
the laughter or fear

rain or cement:

my thirty-sixth year

In the Rear-View Mirror of the Finning Cat

> Under the skin is a huge rubbish heap of crumbled congealed
> magma and dead bodies, pressed into stone over countless
> millions of years.
> —Edward Hyams, *The Changing Face of Britain*

the first bones it unearthed were fresh:
heaved pets   the rattling carriages of birds
traces of human foetus   recent death

you can ignore this close archaeology he thinks
and the weighted cat carves farther into this hill
the underpinning of the old site of Strathcona
his burrowing part of an effort to relieve
a traffic problem: dissecting Edmonton's valley
walls into efficient corridors   knifing deeply
into its exfoliate past

but as the weeks wore on   and he increasingly inward
the low fall sun   the vacuum of the headphones
buried him inside the cab   the only point of contact
that squared castiron jaw extending beneath him
churning up more and more bones farther in

as if it were his jaw

and his eyes bore into the hill in front of him
saw the skeletal death emerge before it was hoisted
clinging   tendrilled history   over his head
sifting down like reasonable patterns into trucks
drawing up behind him to receive this freighted past
saw part of   then the full force of   the Old Vision:

primeval Sponge: ironic   inverted Babel
we dance our straining jig upon   our feet kissed
by its growing   decayed suction   smacking
our leaps forever deeper   downward into some thing:

a world of after-images

of the Worm

laughing dancers sway   hoist faces upward
into sun   half men   half meal
only the torsos twisting in the delight of eyes
while the old jaw works away   draws
the tableau down into the calcium ritual:
a last dream of sponges   final ironies   alive
by empty spaces   once the shouting dancers themselves
now a quiet vacuum of this breathing   undulating thing
fed by negatives   in its own dry way   alive

it was shortly after this assignment that he'd go
to the Strathcona Bar too often   sit there
comfortable in the patronising indifference of
his future: lilting in the students' laughter

it was their bar   their dance now

tap his anemic foot on the sponge of the broadloom
slapping spilt beer to the persistent clumsy jaw of the juke box

his head an unearthed hill

excerpt from Facing the Gardens

    for Allan Forrie

the soul turns in its gardens for gardens

for so long I simply moved past them
gardens in rear-view mirrors on highways

—an erratic indrawn prairie town
shimmering its greens two miles off the highway
its bleached totems encased in foliage
what you imagine as the simple grace of
hoses and sprinklers   white picket fences
a summer rodeo   young men and women
in gingham and hats and jeans chewing straw
lovers in the long grass by the nuisance grounds

or the mottled green avenues of mountain towns
plump and excessive in their fake Austrian
English or American facades for tourists
bundled into narrow passes or valleys
leaning together for strength
sly buoyant and rough people
easy with their land   its sexuality
easy with themselves—

I moved past them
never understood those gardens
though I dreamed of them

and my garden

what was being grown
was often passed by too

and after all the bullshit
the lies late at night on the couch
when my hand reached out for
another beer or a rye
elated in its own mindless energy
its momentary deceptions and defeats
after all these rituals

the peace of gardens

always put off

delayed by the party

the soul turns in its gardens for gardens

I couldn't accept that Al

straight talk from the end of the line kiddo

St. Peter of the crossroads   peering out

into the traffic

1.

                    ...there,
here:) and again cut off,

stranded, lost instead
in these dreams of
dreams: dreams of having
no dreams to love me.
I wake up out of them slowly and
end up sitting here on the couch,
blinking back at the valley and
the town so early in the morning,
can't shake the dreams, the sensation
of separation in them, a loss they
carry like dreams can and
do sometimes.

This is so bad not even waking hours
like this one in a small blue
café can relieve an absence
in the dreams: a distance

from objects and the loss of
love in that: the very thing Plath
found she couldn't stand
waiting for: nothing

flaring at my elbow on

these heavy days of rain:

no sun, not even the horses
that often rescue me,

nothing.

3.

I could pull out the booze and lose
some distance like a sure bet, even if
on those horses that have deserted
me, have faded into the pale light of
noon:

Pull out the booze and diminish
diminishment even,   reach ground
zero: the distance, closed abruptly.

But closed so perfectly you
become what you see and forget that
love was even needed.   You become an
object now yourself, swimming in a
sea the horses have abandoned for
something sweeter, and they're
pulling away suddenly in a scattered
line that leaves you behind, that

forgets you had an eye: the rye

can do this, no

problem.

5.

Of course, there is a rind of anger that protects love.
It's invisible mostly, and encloses the soft pliant heart in a
cerebral ceramic fired by time and a masonry of measurements
that take us off guard, throw us off until we can't believe
we'd stoop to such harsh and ludicrous accountings or
trimmings off the wheel, such intense heat,
the final price paid.

And you're tempted to whisper, "Beware the hopeless
movie of gentleness," lest it turn on you finally, its
pathetic lenses whirring footage of the big
error outwards for everyone to see:

pitiless hope for kindness set against the
mind's measurements, turns out, sometimes,
faked gesture, less honest than anger

itself, than fear, than the shattered rinds
these horses' hooves have crushed in

their cantilevered exits.

6.

You can discipline the eye to turn away from
need, turn flat out into the self instead, ignoring
even richer fields in order to protect itself from

collapsing only outwards, into *other,* seeking
something there, too, maybe, but destroying
something else as well, even accidentally. Even

that. I don't know anymore, these incurled
hesitations so unconcrete and yet, looking
down at my skin, the pores in it, the mirrors

there, then at this oak table top, the glass in
that window I'm staring through, the side-
walks crazy with leaves and the thin smells

of late autumn blinking back at me and
my head alert suddenly and breathing
again, even that, fading.

7.

The junction of the eye and the heart, that crossing,
like directions in a maudlin old blues song—*at the corner of*
Fifth and Argyle, babe!—is where I want to live forever,
whatever that means.

These times so laden with the selfpromoting safeties of
irony and another kind of stylized distance, manufactured
as imagery, persona, mask, so fiercely competitive you
can't help tiring of all this bullshit, this earnest-
ness, these handoverhand, hard-on insecurities
that define competition: just what we

need more of now like a hole in the
fucking head, these jokes we've

become the strut for cool, for knowledge,
slick and packaged ruses of distance, all
roads covered and tracked, known
apparently, all roads paraded as maps
of discovery, now old hat, maps of

some big hole being filled is all:
maps of restlessness, need, and pathetic

bones of loneliness on parade.

What's become of my generation:
bones on parade.

9.

And on some mornings, on your
way back from the blue café,
fragile as rice paper, you find your-
self in both suns accidentally,
your body breathing, your
brown boots flat on the cement,
the death of fall so
rich in your ears and
nose, stuffing itself so
deeply down your throat,
you laugh out loud and
remember some vaguely
parallel junction from
childhood, maybe walking
across the tracks up
to 99th Street in the rain,
maybe wondering who you'd
turn out to be in thirty
years, this older man
walking towards you now,
grinning innocently in
a cobalt sun, the tumbling
chaos of hooves accompanying
his innocence down the street
while you stare into this future
breathless and happy to think
you'd have the chance to'
simply *be* a man walking down
a street in a late fall rain sleek
in red and blue leaves, yellow
with mirrors jumping up
at him, loving him,

the man and the street
dreamed by horses you

can only hear vaguely

galloping in your heart,

boy.

Weightless

I drive around the city like everybody else. I clean out the side-compartments
in the dark crevices and seams of the door of my car where I crumple up chocolate
bar wrappers and stuff them sometimes. On other days I can get organized
enough to wash and vacuum the whole thing creating a brand new world
of car in an hour. And I walk on the cement sidewalks in my sandals
and feel the heat of these sunny spring days through the leather and through
my exposed toes. I walk past the enamel-painted frames of the windows
leading into my favourite café and order the usual the usual the usual,
lugging my take-out coffee onto the charcoal streets, squinting
into the afternoon sun, gripping the steering wheel with real
hands, real flesh, drop by the bank, take some money out, pay some
bills, put some money in, all the usual stuff, all the usual stuff,
and drive up onto the shaded asphalt of my own driveway, turn
the car off, breathe in the heavy tree-scented air, see the lush
gardens she has made, feel the wood of the gate as it creaks
open, reach down to look into the eyes of my loyal dog who
loves me, sense myself anchored in all this, and walking
through my back door and into my home where everything
sits where it's supposed to, heavily and solemnly as my
life, I feel myself begin to thin out in the world, through
the ceiling of this solid house, away from the heart's
gravity, and up over the grey-shingled roof that
covers and protects everything I love, and into
these blue skies (which aren't really blue when
you're ascending, but hard to nail down, hard
to describe), now substance-less in an ether
you're examining, so far away from
my care...*throw me back*, I gasp,
throw me back...unhook me from
this eerie other element and heave
me back down there where I can
swim and love and turn into a dust
that doesn't frighten me.

Gabrielle, Jumping for Joy

Don't know where this one's going to go, but I saw my niece Gabrielle last night
on the landing between the stairs, excited about driving down from Edmonton, thrilled
to be visiting here, be on her way downstairs to the sliding glass doors where
she knew the pool was waiting. After she'd given me the obligatory hug
and smile, had answered a few meaningless questions about the drive
and how long it had been, she looked away, her eyes glazed over
in abstraction, and jumped up involuntarily, into the height
of the air above the landing where you could go up or down,
lifted herself off the ground, her arms wrapped tightly
around her small, eleven year old frame—right into
the air—and in the middle of this ecstasy,
in the fractions of its ascent and descent, our eyes
locked in a distance that is not necessarily
the same world we think it is and I
was happy to have been
there to see her
and be dragged
by her into this
fiercer world
we sometimes
forget to find,
even though
it is at
the heart
of the one
we see.

Driving down the asphalt later, the soft swooshing sounds
of summer everywhere around me like water in the indigo air, the fluorescent lights
of the gas station flickering like fish into the streaks of imperfection
on my night windshield, and the muffled, sliding sounds of skateboards
on the concrete loops in Polson Park playing a staccato polyrhythm
to my heart, stones on the bottom pulsing against the water
above them, I kept seeing Gabrielle on the staircase,
suspended between going up
and going down, an incarnation
of fins and water.

Taking Jude Out For Breakfast On A Sunny Spring Sunday In Summerland, Thirty Years After God

O God of my lost Catholic childhood, hiding in whatever dark corner of those edgy
years I flung myself into so flatly out there on my sidewalks it's a wonder
there's anything *left*, and even knowing you will never assume the form you
once had in my smiling, earnest years, a trust just above the freckles and loose grin,
and admitting my world transformed into *this one here*, the one I'm in now, the one
my body loves, and though I never did this body any favours—even so—I still
think of a wheel of time, the revolution on those clanging, dusty Edmonton
streets, hustling across Whyte Avenue in a February wind, swanning
into Uncle Albert's Pancake House—before franchises, before enclosed
shopping malls—our first introduction to sophistication maybe (we thought),
going out to a restaurant on a Sunday morning, Christine clutching my left
hand, our faces fresh from Mass at St. Joseph's Chapel on the campus,
Father Pendergast in full, soft flight behind us now, the two of us mincing
along Whyte Avenue in a cool wind, as young as we would ever be, our
bodies slim willows moist in a vague pre-spring it seems looking back
now, our shadows cast in front of us on the pale cement,
us trying to interpret those forms dancing in front of us against
the grey, who those people might become in their lives, dark kisses
stretching before us, back-lit by a Catholic God above
and behind us whose long fingers spun fragile threads
connected to our hearts, and shortly to be severed as we
would spin alternately away from both our selves
and that soil we'd been planted in, away into this
room here, its white walls, its peace, even its loony
longing to return to those streets sometimes, but
its firm smile that *this* is enough, *this* its own vertical
light, no strings, no fingers, just a heart beating
in a dark it can take most of the time—
but even so, O God of my long lost
Catholic childhood, *listen*:

lift off the layers of hate that descend
upon us like cages, lift this sour angry light
off the streets so there is no shadow, so
we walk in a flat, translucent dignity
over streets of gold, then re-
turn to the moist, dark soil
we came from, the real soil,
enough.

Molecular Cathedral

This was the poem I didn't want to write, the scary poem that insists
self-interest is the origin for each human action and you have to either
acknowledge that or you're in big trouble and, of course, we don't want
to admit this might be true; we've got way better stories to tell, movies
to make, tearful TV specials to watch on slow Monday evenings
in the fall—but *there ya go!* It's like reading Richard Ford's *Wildlife*
or Céline or Vonnegut on certain days and then trying
to go about living a normal life knowing most of our narratives
of normal are only wild dreams of neo-platonic perfects
selling us the very world our selfishness thinks
it needs to protect and destroy itself at the same
strange time: a bloodied intersection we're
left standing in, the crossroads Robert Johnson
sings about, where we are both consuming
and consumed. *Holy Crap!*

This is the poem I dream about at night restless in my half-sleep,
full of guilt and self-loathing, the poem that saves me from myself,
blesses me with some alternative, whispers redemption into my left
ear while a right hand hovers above my forehead with holy
oil to anoint me so I can get up and walk into the day
with an innocence I might not otherwise find.
It's a dream of primal connection where eyes
look on me with love and forgive me everything.

So how does the poem resolve its own tensions and oppositions?
How can the poem resolve selfishness and connection to others
and the brutal green limits that gird these fields of time and matter? How can
we accept this vessel of flesh and bone, this home, and not destroy it and allow
it to turn in a bright field of other dancing bodies, occasionally intersecting, touching,
alive in a primal *presence* and a longing past safety and hunger, for replication, yes,
but for something more, too, something not anticipated maybe, always a surprise,
something that moves us past our selves in a whoosh of logic we cannot
see or sense until we are standing there, unaccommodated
in an open field, staring both at the intricate web of skin
on our hands and the blue, blue air of summer we're gulping
down like water against the heat, this incarnation we are,
the word made flesh, a molecular cathedral straining
within itself, its medieval, gothic balances
and counter-turns and arches and cross-bracing,

its unimaginable architecture a gift
that *requires* selfishness as a *pledge* not
a betrayal of love: the harder
path even.

Carpenter

The finches, chickadees and wrens have wildly returned this morning
in the bird-feeder outside our front window. I repaired it yesterday. The birds
had worn it out over the winter so it was teetering
to the rhythm of their pecking, and threatening to fall beneath
their weight and the shifting weight of the snow and rain as well.
So I took a few hours and found some old 3/4" slats and some cast-
away 3/8" plywood.

                       I began drawing out what I imagined
I needed on a piece of paper. This is always a good move for me
as it discloses, early on, mistakes in logic and architecture
I will invariably make. By drawing it out, I visualize precisely what
I'm trying to do and anticipate errors by seeing through the sketch
to the real. *Always interesting when you look back on it.* And it all
worked out, this small making. I'm pleased. The birds seem
happy.

                       But I find myself standing
on the lawn now, staring at this thing I've made, amazed, and another
version of me standing even further back, watching the first,
is muttering, laughing: *yes, it's amazing, for you've made some
thing out of the stuff of this world, and you have, for once,
joined it perfectly.* And there it is again, this mystery
of joining, of intersections, corners, fits, so
damn important in everything we do, each
small jazz symphony we might
construct, for example,
or song we might want
to sing in the middle
of a night, or poem
to the earth, our dust,
or this thought
here, or this
join and
hinge:
you.

Intersections

1.

It's what you begin to see as you grow older and it's not
that it's a surprise. Standing, having a smoke in the gravel
parking lot of a truck-stop in Merritt, you remember sifting
through the bookstore offerings earlier, back in Vancouver,
registering the obvious glare of new voices, new techniques,
other generations whispering up behind yours, and you had
to accept the seduction was already *over*, past you, and any
of your pronouncements about the lure of fame and glory
were, in fact, precisely accurate: your voice was *not* going
to announce itself, or even whisper, or if whispering,
it was going to be the tiny swoosh of a wren or a sparrow
flitting past your head in this truck-stop, the sound of pines
creaking like looms in the wind, *that* subtle, *that* soft, *that* in-
tricate really, or a saxophone reeling back into its improvised
maelstrom of gravity in the middle of a piece, stretching
and winging away into the inside of the wind, the ear of the bird,
the heart of the pine.
     That you are here and as planted
and as green as everything else and *that* is the gift itself, *that*
communion of air, of earth, of water. Fire in your head
as raging—as bill bissett would say—as raging as the ear
of the wind, the heart of the bird, the inside of the pine, all
one and raging in an inarticulate rush of breath and pulse
and fibre, immediate, immanent, all old testament god stirring
on gravel, slouching, ready, there, the bellows of the lungs meshed
through the cortex to the lips to the reed, all the deep, fluted,
sharp bird and wind and pine notes flapping into the air
as themselves, as hymn to the nothing-really-matters-but-this-
moment-now song, being *in* it, being.
     Your body
pivots over the rough, pebbly asphalt, the wind creases
and folds as air, the long stretches of bird and pine
and sage fall away in intersecting planes of matter and you've
been deposited as Adam in this creaking, folding, billowing,
crazy and imperfect paradise, standing squarely, singing
through the lips of Eden.

2.

the care-
ful turn-
ing turn-
ing turn
of tongue
and pa-
lette and
grunt and
groan of
words that
need to
try to say
what it
is, having
to take a
picture of
the pic-
ture of
the picnic
more than
having the
picnic it-
self: that
fear that
forces us
to arrest
it while
it's mov-
ing. Let it
be. *Don't.*
Don't!

3.

did you give your care
to something else? Your focus
and attention? Did you
forget your self?

4.

the tree the bird the wind
and you there, too, your in-
drawn wilderness accelerating
into the other, two songs
one song until the black, dark,
charcoal silence of the earth in which,
on which, other equal songs
braid the sweet-sweet marbled
clay and air and water: combustion
engine everywhere aflame until
all weaving ends in light

5.

Play that song.
Play it again.
Now, *improvise.*

Light

> I set my feet with care in such a world.
> —William Stafford

Walk out into the kitchen's morning
light sifting through the half-opened
smudged window and I wonder how
do these surfaces become me
become the life I lead and lead
me on, invisible threads
in a web of ritual, a design
that's itself only half-opened
to light sometimes, always
half-hidden, too, hiding
another kind of light in
me, I suspect.

And it's when the two
fields of light collide
in a crazy sideways surprise,
when some corridor prism
rushes up through the blood
to the eyes to the mind
wrestling with itself,
and is caught turning in the other,
wilder light that these two
forests mirror one
another and all grids
and order collapse into a geometry
that cannot be envisioned
but simply, wildly, is.

You turn a faucet, you
feel the chrome handle
while another part of you
reaches for the coffee beans
and all surfaces, outside and in,
are illuminating this instant
of pure glee, pure surface,

the skin of any god you might
want to name, or any dignity
that has avoided the light
so far in the dark.

Matins 2, Long Beach, October 25, 2014

Medieval or renaissance beach and ocean and wide sun-flooded sand
stretches of beach flats—me walking out on them a new man: not just
because I survived a quadruple bypass…but because of me, how I grew
up, when I grew up: *that* kind of a new person in a new world. New eyes.
De-romanticized but still flooded (as the sand) with a bright wonder you
almost have to squint into to survive it is so beautiful. You almost wince
from it. A kind of pain. And yet or *but* yet, I have this guide—this Welsh
Springer spaniel named Mosey—to lead me out onto these dazzling sand
flats and into a new world and sun and rain and no enclosures caused
by the mind (Blake's mind-forged manacles) enclosures of sentiment,
patriotism, false honor, dysfunctional loyalties, empty gestures of love
instead of love itself, instead of clarity itself, instead of sight itself. If we
could only stay out here in the wind, or never forget standing here. While
the surging tides pull us out and draw us in and we match that surge
pulse for pulse, big-hearted, lungs full before the final dark, that all-
encompassing dark love that is another kind of full. We are truly blessed,
wonder-filled, wonder-full…

Matins 3, November 4, 2014

…praise and gratitude…funny how these old Catholic words might
come back to 'literally' haunt me…praise and gratitude…I'm out walking
Mosey this morning in the early morning humid mild fall Okanagan air…
everything quiet…Mosey's head swaying below me from side to side, the
rhythmic swinging encased by the plastic cowl he's been wearing since
last Thursday when he had his significant operation…and my instinctive
voice whispering, "That's a good dog…good old Mosey…" side to side
as well, just above his radar, just above mine, too, because I'm not even
aware of my voice until another human being crosses our path and I
become, abruptly, self-conscious (but only momentarily), then lapse back
into our side-to-side ritual once again…but the smell of the morning, its
textures of concrete and damp grass and maple leaves collecting in every
seam out here…soft and light and beautiful, whatever that means…but
alive…pulsing…praise and gratitude…lately, in that other landscape—my
head—a tumble of confusion and sadness and a kind of flatness I rarely
experience…a flatness *like* sadness, but not the same…more cruel and
less sweet than sadness…I know it's connected to something that shifted
permanently in me when I got sick…I know it has to do with my getting
a glimpse and a feel for the end of things…a kind of darkness I had never
imagined before…a crazy, desperate leaving of everything behind…a
silence that cannot be fathomed or, even, heard until you're embraced
by it…and it's not all negative, though it sounds like it…not at all…but
it can't be artificially redeemed or idealized or romanticized either…it is
beyond what we try to resolve through words like positive and negative…
it will have nothing to do with either of those words…instead, it's just
waiting there like a great yawning charcoal vacuum…and you walk
around in the face of it, and that walking around in the face of it affects
everything else you're doing, all your dreams, your petty enthusiasms,
your loves, your friendships, your relations and relationships…it lays
on a skin of qualification, of hesitancy, of, not horror, but an almost
appalling clarity that has to do with a parallel flatness in what we call
the real or ordinary world…nothing like it…so you're stumbling along
the street with this cowl around your body, your small dog leading you
through this, your guide…and you're thinking, "OK. I can do this I
guess," and another voice slips into the proceedings from the sidelines
somewhere—in an unexpected rush of metaphysics and magic—and
whispers, "Praise and gratitude, boy. Praise & gratitude." And you squint
into the eastern morning sun and gulp down its logic and think, *yes*, it *is*
praise and gratitude…that's what I'm here for: to love and acknowledge

love, and praise and acknowledge the loves of the body, too, the elements, the micro-presences of whatever we used to mean by words like god, get down on my knees again near the end of my life, and in the face of this wheezing abundance, whisper *thank you*…here, on my knees in the early morning back alley, my eyes welling up in joy, not sorrow, the cowl lifting itself off to the light…my small dog a kite on a string, a pressure I can barely feel I am so unsubstantial…

Matins 5, January 11, 2015

Walking into the face of God…that's the recurring image/voice/whisper/
blessing I kept getting this morning as Mosey and I trudged south
through Marshal Fields, past the airport and along the creek to the lake.
Small but continuous & firm tracks through the snow…Mosey bounding,
me always balancing, balancing, gauging the surprises in the foundation
path caused by the snow, a buoyant hesitancy defining the pilgrimage…
pilgrimage…into the face of God…the image I kept getting was of a three-
dimensional cut-out in the landscape and sky…if I held my balancing
arms and legs out in a certain, clever, mysterious way, I would pass
through a key-lock into paradise…walking right into and through the
skin of God, the face of God…it's funny because I just started reading a
book about Celtic wisdom last night—*Anam Cara* by John O'Donohue—
and one of the first points he makes is that for the Celts there was no
distinction between landscape and subjectivity…there were one and the
same…so consciousness walks into consciousness and vice versa…how
that all works with Don McKay's notion of wilderness and domesticity…
so, when I say that I walked into the face of God, I may be saying that the
most undomesticated part of me, the truly wildest part of me, walked into
the most undomesticated part of God…

Matins 8, April 9, 2015

Because my brother Michael sent me a clip of Nancy Wilson, singing...

In a YouTube clip of an ancient 1964 TV appearance, Nancy Wilson performs her version of "The Very Thought Of You," and I'm listening so hard to her phrasing, her breath, until, finally, the music, as sumptuous as the melody of this song *is*, surrenders its lovely and considerable machinery over to the mere voice telling an impossibly intimate story. I think of poetry, naturally, and the function of surprise. I remember reading somewhere once that Michael Ondaatje had confessed he 'wanted to be changed' when he read a poem. That's what he expected. I used to regale my writing students with this anecdote because I thought it was so beautiful and so frightening at the same time. Over the years, I suspect I refined his comment so that each time I sit down to write, I try to write until I surprise myself. Just look at Nancy Wilson leaning forward now into the mic, gesturing with both arms after singing the intro, suspended over the real start of the song now...just watch her body, her shoulders, as she lilts for the first time into the words, 'The very thought of you.' Incredible suspension. And in spite of any predictably contrived effects around it and in it, her body collapses at this very point into a sure, almost trance-like improvisation of the words, and her gorgeous, misshapen, always fluctuating mouth goes on to twistingly tell the wonderful story of her love. I cannot believe the way she handles, as a singer, word clusters like, 'the mere idea of you.' The weight on idea. The way she draws out the idea of idea until the very charcoal limits of my own spring morning here fifty-three years later are swept away in a spring rinse of thought, of carbon and time and generation and regeneration and ideas of ideas, and as the world collapses outside my window into its very limit, Nancy Wilson's voice is a thin, reedy balsam from somewhere behind or beneath everything else I am letting go of, all that bulky fumbling thinking as, instead, I watch my hand stretching itself away from and toward the release of everything it used to touch and try to claim. Of you. Whatever in the dust of it you are. The very.

Matins 20, March 31, 2016

Joining. Joinery. "Joinery is a part of woodworking that involves joining together pieces of timber or lumber, to produce more complex items." Seams. Stitches. Joins. We were talking about art the other morning, Jude and I, and I blurted out that everything had to do with seams and joins. Predictably ridiculous comment, right out of the blue. Typical. *Non sequitur*. But I had been thinking for days about the *construction* of things, the *composition* of things, from concrete structures to abstract structures, and I think I had begun to understand something I had been working on instinctively, for years, in my own writing: the intricate, subtle and almost frighteningly important art of joinery. Knowing where the breaks are, the seams are. Knowing how to allow panels to exist side by side and still stand, joined, independent but linked. These things *are* important. The glue of structure. Where the breaks are, the seams are. And just as crucial, where they are in the world *before* they exist as the rhythm for an artistic object. So you think, for example, of the simple notion of story, of narrative. And you stare into the original circuitry *in the world*, and then you imagine an alternate, complimentary, or more magical *corresponding* circuitry *in the art*. Another, beautiful world. And you imagine where the seams are, the breaks, the joins. Same thing in poetry. Where these things are in the world, and then, where they might be in that other, crazy, but gorgeous world of, literally, earthly delights. *Incarnation*. The word made flesh. *Hoc est enim corpus meum.*

Three arborists are over in the house behind us this morning, dismantling a one-hundred-year-old maple that has become too old, too weak in its limbs after years of inexpert pruning. You know how it is. It happens all the time, even here in a valley of orchards. They are disassembling the tree from top to bottom, a reversal of its slow growth, whatever that means. They will take it down to the nub of its roots, even pulverizing the roots. A complete deconstruction. A collapse. An unfolding. Erasure. One hundred years collapsing around me in a meticulously orchestrated circuitry of structure and joins. "Counselling decision, decision..." William Stafford's sharp swallows swerving, "flaring and hesitating, hunting for the final curve" in his wondrous poem, "The Well Rising." Decisions. Where the seams are. The joins, the breaks. Decisions.

On the wall to the left of my desk, I have a beautiful black and white photo of my grandfather, John Hugh Brown, the man I was named after. In the photo my grandfather is in his eighties and he is in his office, fixing a

clock. After his own jewelry store collapsed in 1929 because of the fall of
the stock markets in North America, my grandfather worked for the CPR,
fixing clocks. He also refereed professional hockey in the Maritime league,
and was so good at it that when he was retiring they got him to referee
a game between Boston and Montreal. That kind of eye, eh? Something
precise in his gaze that allowed him to calibrate things. Of course, all these
possible metaphors are now beginning to pull away from one another's
logic. *Non sequitur.* But regardless of such dissolution occurring in my
own attempt to force a join, it is true to say that one hundred years ago
today, my grandfather, my mother's father, was a young married man
living with his wife and two daughters in Moncton, New Brunswick. My
mother, Adrienne, would be born into this family six years later, in 1922.
She would give birth to me in 1948. The limbs. The seams. The joins. This
architecture. Collapsing. Decision, decision.

Hoc est enim corpus meum.

"I place my feet/with care in such a world."

Matins 32, Wednesday, October 12, 2016

So the smallest thing—wiping the countertop to the left of the stainless steel sink with a J-cloth, the J-cloth just freshly squeezed in a piping hot rinse—the smallest gesture becomes a celebration simply because you are *in* it, you are part of every thing, you are alive. And you've just realized that soon, in time, that might not be the case. So it's the pleasure, the dignity in each thing as it unfolds in the air, as it becomes its own architecture in time and space, as it becomes a molecular cathedral, like you…like you. And then nothing. You have to let it all roll forward at that point without you, something you also love the idea of because it is a part of love to understand the borders, the edges, the way things start and stop…a very big part of love.

excerpt from Prague Spring: Twelve Cubist Sonnets

Prague Poem 3

When you set forth in words like this, it's not as if you *will* the words to
a final logic so the words become a simulacrum of something—the way a
photograph seems to stop time, or a portrait copies part of something.

It's that you trust the words, like music, by starting out in the earth
ground of the body, in the concrete field the body is registering around
itself, will move into both the body and that electrical field around it, and
by some bizarre circuitry, reach beyond both to that other matrix that is
also there, that resists ordinary logic, that rushes the heart and the mind
and surprises both, and is as close as we can get to saying what the breath
of being is.

So it's not that the words copy.

They are set forth babbling, as probe.

They find things. They open things up. They become something.

[...the young woman feeling sorry for me in the bakery earlier, forgiving
me my awkward lack of confidence in *her* words, *her* language, and
grinning at me so generously beyond both sets of words, she restored
me to the bakery, pulled me back into my body standing in front of her
from a point of view that was from farther on down the line, when I was
already looking *back* at this moment and making fun of myself in it, full
of swagger of course, the *traveller*. The *raconteur*. She rescues me from
that and insists on placing me here, now, in *this* garden, my feet on the
ground, her many gestures a cubist blessing from all sides simultaneously.
Who would have thought that when I was starting out here? This is no
trip into the ordinary...]

Prague Poem 6

That's what happens, maybe, when you ease into your 60s: you begin to
see more. I just saw this man in his 70s—all dressed up, likely headed to
the bank, looking pretty spiffy. He was walking along the street opposite
the window I'm staring through in this coffee shop I've found at the
corner of Kosi and Kolkovně in the old Jewish Quarter of Prague. He
was checking his pants for something, doing something he was certain
of. Then, abruptly, he stopped walking and, instead, stared up at the sky
for no reason. He spotted something of interest up there and he began
to squint at it, shading his eyes with his right hand on his forehead,
stretching his mouth out wide in the process as if it might help the
concentration, staring up at whatever it was. People just kept milling past
him in a wild flow. Life went on. But he'd interrupted himself looking at
something. Maybe for the first time. It's possible.

Of course, I was watching *him*.

And you?

That's what it feels like. Being a kid again. Seeing things for the first time.
Watching the physics of the world around you disclose itself law for law,
surface for surface, wheel for interlocking wheel.

Like the circular, waxed cardboard seals on glass milk bottles back in
the '50s in Edmonton. The bottle was left on your front doorstep by the
delivery man who drove a square, yellow van. In the winter the bottles
would crack open in the cold if you didn't bring them in as soon as they
were delivered, and the first thing to give was the circular cardboard seal.
It'd be staring up at you at an odd angle supported by a churn of frozen
milk that looked chalky and spongy. Some days, there'd be a glass bottle
of chocolate milk there, too, and you'd all go crazy! What a surprise!

Before plastic.

Before franchises.

Before everything was processed.

Before you stopped seeing.

Look! Here! It's spring!

Bridal wreath is breaking out everywhere behind these stone walls. It's as if everything around you has been imagined by Derain and in the snap of two fingers, has become three-dimensional.

It's Prague!

Pivot!

Prague Poem 7

I love each of my brothers and sisters. Four brothers, two sisters. We
grew up in a fierce bond that cannot be broken, but our adult lives,
and our different abilities to survive and enjoy them, are each of them
unique, and, as a result, sometimes each of us feels perpetually stranded,
each one of us looking for phantom limbs. And they're out there, those
limbs. We must not forget that. They're out there intensely, and they
whirl in a perpetual motion matrix that is always unfolding as the past,
where love was first discovered, and where it was unconditional. The fact
that we have been carried by these waters away from one another—into
other loves and other families—is a sea that surrounds the first matrix,
but doesn't alter it. These two oceans whirl, counter-clockwise, one
around the other, alternating their movements like a beneficent, poised
machine, some medieval clock clicking and clacking its way through the
mornings, afternoons and evenings of our small delights and sorrows and,
throughout it all, separated islands of recognition and affection. *If it could
only be like this! If words could simply crack open these riddles sometimes
and be the balm of love, its core.*

Hey, it's spring in Prague. I love each and every one of you. We will
love one another beyond the dark carbon kiss that will lay each one of
us down to rest eventually in the earth—all the double machinery and
water in those moments seeming to caterwaul and collapse into another
kind of dust, too—even then, and beyond what seems a ruined landscape
of objects that are suddenly only partial things, reverberating beyond
that even into another physics: an impossible poem that must reach out
beyond itself, admitting everything, to be possible.

Prague Poem 8

So you get, finally, to love. The texture of love in this strange, new city with her, this baroque, art nouveau, cubist dream of a city that seems to possess the familiarity that dreams have, that Kafka-esque tableau wherein you accept everything: of *course* this is Prague and I'm *in* it. Of *course*. I get it.

I have watched you for thirty-four years as you transformed in your body and stayed the same. *Exactly*. I have watched you turn and pivot through the many red dances we've been drawn into, toe to toe, our feet like hands.

The rain is falling against the skylight in the living room of this apartment on Bílkova this evening. Though the rain is thick with grey, the sky is also bright. There's a sun close by. The pigeons coo and crackle across the red clay tiles. A siren rises and subsides a mile away, beyond the Jewish Quarter.

You are asleep down the hall, your body a complex Russian doll of encasements of interlocking times and versions of you—not as chronological time, but as different bodies of you that lean into different grasses for embraces. You lie there so slight, but contain all those fronds of you that are also there, sleeping, and dreaming.

In one of those dreams a child, a young girl, is painting on watercolor paper in a white room. The child is methodically dipping a brush in then out of an old pickle jar full of discolored water, careful to squeeze out just the right amount of water from the brush hairs each time on the lip of the glass. And then the child dips the moist brush into the bright-red tablet in her metal painting case and begins to move the brush on the rough-surfaced bone-white and slightly damp paper. A bird whistles somewhere through an open window. The heavy smell of spring lilacs invades the room. The girl is smiling. She is dreaming herself a princess in an old European city, asleep in a tower, awaiting the prince. He is climbing a dark, circular staircase to reach her. He is always climbing those stairs.

Yesterday we toured the Jewish Museum and Synagogue and, most marvelous, the ancient Jewish cemetery here in Josefov. In the museum we saw a room of children's art that had been rescued from the Terezín Concentration Camp during World War Two. A small white card beneath each of the paintings indicated whether that child had survived or not.

I watched you pause at each of these paintings. You have taught so many children art over the years I have known you. I watched you disappear into those paintings, those lives. You knew instinctively what was being whispered and celebrated in each case.

Eventually, hand in hand, we descended the stone spiral stairs of the synagogue and out of the gallery and down onto the bright streets of Prague. We had coffee in the Franz Kafka Café. We walked the cobblestone streets as young lovers might, transformed by love, by being *in the world*.

I am sitting just down the hall from you right now, writing. You are asleep, dreaming. I am always climbing stairs to reach you. Those children. Dark spiral staircases, everywhere. Lilacs. I am the heavy, rough paper. Your eyes see something unfolding on me: you are smiling at a bright-red narrative. The dewlap brush hairs caress my stretching skin and it all begins to happen again. Of *course*. I get it.

This Golden Dusk, Jude Clarke, 2007

Afterword

Molecular Cathedral: Consciousness and Things

For my very own Matisse, the painter Jude Clarke

Jake Kennedy has constantly amazed me in the process of putting this book together. He has made the selections of poetry from an over forty-year history of publication, and he has written a dazzling and generous essay that provides a prescient overview of that long arc of composition. What he sees in his essay is so wide-ranging, intricate, complex, and human, especially in his consideration of the visions and forms of the poems. That's the thing for me, eh? Vision and form. Both are so hard to see in any instance of setting up a long view of a writers' work, but Jake lets us see both all the way through, right from the beginning. My job here is to respond to what he has done, and I have to say it has been tricky in the face of such obvious care and skill. But I will contribute something whimsical in order to honour what Jake has done and to hint, too, at some of the literary ground I see in my own past that led me to crucial decisions I would eventually make about vision and form in my writing. I will build something quirky that might complement his overview in an eccentric way: a thumbnail sketch, as Matisse might have drawn, a gesture sketch, improvised, immediate, full of loose distortion, but, in its own way, maybe perfect. It will be a sketch of the most private part of me that wasn't always trying to be responsible, or trying to please everyone around me by either laughing or apologizing or simply doing things to make life work more smoothly maybe, but that part of me instead that was mostly concealed, mostly quiet, and mostly looking for something indifferent out there that might lift me and carry me through everything else that was also happening, and allow me the space I needed to make things.

[That part of me that was concealed was the one each of us have, but don't trust very much sometimes, or are afraid of in some vague way because of how the body interprets the word "selfish." It is, however, a fundamental part of the self that makes things happen in the soul, that invents a clockwork gold and steel and polished leather metaphysical harness that can carry us gently forward, blind but sure about the perilous movement anyway. That part of the self.

It is the part that gets grounded in its own poetics early on and stays that way and allows those poetics to expand, refine, and recreate themselves by launching attempts at beauty with no hesitation about what it's reaching for, only that strange inexplicable rush instead. And that rush is almost impossible to see.]

When I was growing up in Edmonton in the '50s and '60s, I walked a lot on the South Side, especially in the fall and the winter months. It seemed strange, even to *me* sometimes. I was a bit self-conscious about it. But I loved walking in the leaves and the snow and thinking about everything. And I knew I couldn't do that with anyone else. It was like praying maybe or meditating or reading Thomas Merton, and I never tired of it. And there were great spots I'd end up in. I especially loved the South Side Public Library which was an old-fashioned red brick two-storey building just off Whyte Avenue on 104th Street. It's still there if you want to see it. When you walked up the granite steps and opened the heavy door, you walked into a bumbling haphazard and eerily ordered cocoon of books and the strong smells of leather and lemon oil and oak trim everywhere and oak desks and bookshelves and nooks and crannies and in the background, the unpredictable algorithm of radiators creaking and whispering and coughing up heat in the winter. I loved the books there. They were an endless thrill for me and still are. I'd sometimes end up in the Edmonton Art Gallery too, which was an old big house across the High Level Bridge just west of 109th Street near the Marchand Apartments in those days. I bet it was run by a society of volunteers. You'd walk in out of the dark afternoon and the snow into this hallowed quiet space that had all these incredible paintings on display. The first thing you noticed was a big rubber sheet next to the door to put your boots on while you were inside. There was always a smattering of the Group Of Seven, Emily Carr, and other more contemporary artists like the young Dorothy Knowles from Saskatchewan, or Jack Bush also from Saskatchewan, or Jack Shadbolt from Vancouver. I remember standing in front of a David Milne painting of an Ontario winter landscape and realizing that the key color in painting snow was, oddly enough, blue. I remember thinking about that when I had looked at some of Clarence Gagnon's paintings the year before as well. That was the trick! Stunning!

And I'd end up on Saturday mornings on the second floor of another ancient building on 101st Street right downtown across from the Metropolitan Five & Dime, and I'd be ascending out of the snow and crazy static of downtown voices and trucks and cars up the long, narrow staircase (with no bends) that led up to the Shepy National School Of Arts where the artist Alex Shepy (Alexis Shepetys) had a vast painting studio with a fifteen-foot ceiling and taught different levels of painting and had at least two gifted assistants who taught junior classes and these were the classes I was taking. I was fifteen and quite a bit older than the other students in my classes, but he'd agreed to slot me into these introductory classes so I could move up to the advanced classes after I was confident enough in some of the fundamentals first, and somehow my mom and dad had found a way to pay for these classes. I wanted to be a painter back then and I loved everything about these lessons. I met Alex Shepy a few times and he was so kind to me in my shyness. He told me he'd come to Edmonton as an immigrant after the war. The second time I visited him he told me that when he was a young man in Lithuania, he'd won a national arts scholarship that gave him the chance to go to Paris for a year to study painting. He wasn't telling me the whole of his story—I suspected he was protecting me in some way—but I could tell everything about his history was complicated, backward and forward through time, maybe especially this new life in Edmonton. Yet he was truly a happy man and a kind man. It was easy to see. "I had the chance to study with Matisse, John," he whispered shyly, almost apologetically, but excitedly too. "Did you?" I replied in my own innocence, "How wonderful!" On my long walk home, I went to the South Side Library and found a heavy, comprehensive book on 20th century European art history. I looked up Matisse, and I stared at the four or five pages of small and larger prints they had of his work. The bold, almost enameled primary colors: the reds and even the blacks. Everything was jumping with life in these paintings, smiling right back out at my boyish, freckled face. And my life changed. As simple as that. I was lost in the faint smells of oak and lemon oil and the uneven chugging of the radiators in the library as my Shakespearean chorus behind me.

This was, in fact, Edmonton after the war: heaven: tough and lucky: modest and sacred. The next Saturday, I was able to ask Mr. Shepy about Matisse and he told me some wonderful and funny stories about working with Matisse, just to help me dial down the myth a bit so I could live with it more comfortably and take it in more humanly. We sat that day and had tea in his red studio room with the Saturday light coming through the window and the snow everywhere outside. We were sitting one floor above other people's voices yelling back and forth down in the street below, and floating through a window he'd left partly open, a warm breeze, almost a chinook, making the white cotton curtains flutter softly against the white, painted window frame. We were sitting in two black rattan chairs. I was in love with being in his world in those moments, though I didn't understand what that meant. It was a Saturday in winter. I'd be playing hockey outside on Tipton Park rink tomorrow afternoon at the same time. Everything would be different then. It was Edmonton. It was a weekend. And then suddenly here I am now, a seventy-four-year-old man sitting in a small room, in British Columbia. It's spring and I'm sitting at a desk in a room full of books and I'm writing this memory out of my own history now: a complicated history, just like Mr. Shepy's.

* * *

In the long run, my love for modern painting, and my desire to become a visual artist, moved from Mr. Shepy's studio over to literature because of my father, Harry Lent, who ended up being my high school English and Latin teacher for grades eleven and twelve at St. Mary's High School on 99th Street on Edmonton's South Side. It's hard to say this in a sentence or two—though I'm comforted by the fact that I have written about my dad in so many poems and stories that what I'm about to say is pretty obvious—but when I sat in his classrooms and watched him teach English Literature or Latin Literature and Language, I was watching a master of both teaching and the materials of teaching: materials that demonstrated the importance of art in our lives. He was truly gifted and it was something to see. He brought art to life in front of us and would improvise silly parodies or simply delight in the buried wit of Shakespeare or Robert Browning in deft little asides so we would believe and understand their importance: "That's my last teacher standing in the hall, looking as if he were alive; I call that piece a wonder now." Or asking us in the middle of teaching *Death of a Salesman*, "What if I told you *I* was Willy Loman?" He had the ability to show us the life *in* the art, the humanity of it.

I don't know exactly what happened to me in my own world of art over time, but I have to say I sure was lucky. I was lucky from the start with mentors and I was equally lucky with the students I got to teach. I used to joke in my last few years of teaching that I was the incarnation of the term "postmodern." But even though they'd laugh and shake their heads, they likely didn't get it; the students were too young to understand what I meant as a long view of change, or how complicated and difficult it was to resolve all those changes in one writer. I was born in 1948, just after World War II ended. I turned 20 in 1968, just at the height of complex cultural and political changes in North America. I tempered and refined my own consciousness in the parody and irony and cynicism that surfaced quite naturally in both content and form in the literary ways of making things in Western literatures in the '50s and '60s. I watched the fields of literary criticism and literary theory change at an exponential rate from the seemingly innocent yet brutal "new criticism" of the early '70s to the equally strident and self-conscious post-structural criticism of the '90s and 2000s, a thirty-year progression that changed almost every significant thing you might want to set about trying to say about literary intention and convention. At the University of Alberta, I got two degrees in literature, the second one focusing on T.S. Eliot's plays. I pursued another degree at York University in a dissertation that tried to illuminate the complex technical *tour de force* that was Malcolm Lowry's novel *Under the Volcano*. I focused on the composition of this novel, especially the concepts of "reification of subjectivity" and the artistic juxtaposition of "consciousness and things" in "stream of consciousness" fiction. From 1971 to 1981, I worked on these issues and I learned so much my head *still* hurts even thinking about it in retrospect. From *A Rock Solid* (1978) and *Wood Lake Music* (1982) on, my own writing would surface out of this intense work on Malcolm Lowry and T.S. Eliot. From the beginning, I knew that neither genre nor hybridity were going to be barriers for me and what I wanted to write; I was learning to work in poetry, fiction, and non-fiction, and to mix them, and was excited to move sideways through genres in order to unearth designs for narrative.

I wanted to place this literary history before you, before saying much else, because all the good things and even bad things that attend my life and career are buried here like an archaeological dig alongside my writing: my insecurities and bungling in terms of the requisite fame and fortune "games"; my own complicated personality, filled with self-sabotage; the fact that I was always an academic as well as a writer; that I was always teaching either literature courses or creative writing courses, not just writing my own writing; that I knew things many writers did not know, especially about contemporary forms; that I knew things many academics could not know, especially about the strain in composition between received structures and improvisation within or without structures; that I was from the west; that I was too damn earnest; that I was an elitist snob; that I was a proletarian cowboy from Alberta; that I was not an alpha male; that I was neither Major Major Major Major *nor* Huple's cat; that I was always a bit hybrid, never completely relaxed or accepted in the world of writers and never completely relaxed or accepted in the world of academics. And, over time, all this borderline/exile territory became OK with me, even healthy, and sometimes epically comic. But I guess the bottom line through it all was that my life was still so lucky and privileged—a life in art in my own country—and I will always be so grateful for such luck and coincidence.

My writing life has been a huge love nourished by three practices: first, the love of writing; second, the love and curiosity and discipline required to strike forms to contain that writing, and finally, the love that held the first two together, the love of teaching new writers about these practices. My advice to anyone taking on this double life of teaching and writing is easy to give, but harder to achieve: this kind of life is both arduous and full of ardour because it is a life of ongoing love, and though it's a hard love in some ways, it is also thrilling, almost ecstatic, and that's what I *really* learned from my mentors and collaborators, writers and teachers like Sheila Watson, Robert Kroetsch, and Don Summerhayes.

Jake Kennedy refers to "both the magic and the ordinariness of consciousness" as two elements that combine in my work. Man, if I could catch both in *any* of my poems or stories, that would mean everything to me. I'm not kidding! And I have to say Kennedy is so right when he speaks of "captured consciousness" and then it echoes back to what he suggested earlier in his essay regarding the role of "static" in both the vision and the forms in my writing. For me, "captured consciousness" and "static" are two sides of seeing what I might say are the subject and object of my sense of the beautiful in the human. The first describes what I'm reaching for that is right in front of me in my life and times, and the second describes what the texture and shape and form of the resulting art might be if I can find it properly and represent it. The latter is why I have been so interested in concepts of spatial form for so long, ways to represent that static as narrative. Succinctly, this is precisely where I wanted to go in my writing from those old Edmonton and Toronto days until now, and it has everything to do with why I felt as a young man that my life in microcosm—that autobiographical field of wonder and beauty that I lived out in Edmonton with my mother and father and brothers and sisters— was a life that needed to be heard and understood by being represented carefully and intimately so its dignity and truths could be appreciated politically, too, and help in the general subversion of hierarchies that have held us back for too long anyway, and which always need to be subverted and exposed for what they are, "real enough." I believe there was a small but consistent vein of mischief in my motives regarding how I had myself experienced our sometimes cruel, always sly and seemingly hidden class system in our so-called, self-congratulatory Canadian culture. It was all about the table and who gets to sit at it. It's still all about that. This is a hard-to-describe but enormously human landscape that I believe both the magic and the ordinariness in my writing are always waging a quiet war against.

Jake Kennedy can see the long haul. That doesn't always happen in cases like this, and boy, am I grateful to him. I have lived my life in art in a certain way that did not expect such a generous, lucid eye to pore over its modest bits and pieces and see how they fit together. So thank you, thank you, Jake. You have given me such a gift and you have opened a door on my work I could never have opened myself. I am thrilled that this book of selected poems has been made, especially by you, to examine some of the fruit of my own writing, and I'm thrilled on another level entirely, by the notion that some young person sitting somewhere in this country having a coffee on a winter Saturday afternoon in a red shopping mall just off the ring road highway, might be inspired by this book to try celebrating his or her or their own life and the texture of that life, both in people and in landscapes, because all those things *should* be caught and celebrated, for that is precisely where beauty always is, not somewhere else.

—*John Lent*

Acknowledgements

A Rock Solid (Toronto: Dreadnaught Press, 1978)
Wood Lake Music (Vancouver: Harbour Publishing, 1982)
Frieze (Saskatoon: Thistledown Press, 1984)
The Face in the Garden (Saskatoon: Thistledown Press, 1990)
Black Horses, Cobalt Suns (Victoria: Greenboathouse Press, 2000)
Cantilevered Songs (Saskatoon: Thistledown Press, 2009)
A Matins Flywheel (Saskatoon: Thistledown Press, 2019)

Author's Note

And here, near the end of my own gratitude, I need to thank so many people, and I know I can't really do that. It won't work because there are, literally, too many people to thank. But you *do* know who you are, and I feel confident about that. I will, however, attempt a short list that is absolutely necessary: Sheila Watson for showing me that I could be a writer in Canada if I really worked first on having something to *say*; Robert Kroetsch for coming into my life as a hero when I was eighteen years old, then as a mentor thirty years later when I was forty-eight and I needed his spirit to help me and he simply showed up out of the blue and did; Don Summerhayes for becoming my on-the-ground mentor in Toronto in the 70s and who taught me what ambiguity meant and how to take Henry James and Walker Evans photographs with words; Don Coles for writing *Forests of the Medieval World*; Don McKay (unbeknownst to him) for being my quiet background model, so steady and frighteningly good in his vision, so persistent in his astonishing work; Alistair MacLeod for taking my breath away in his writing and in his advice; Michael Ondaatje (again unbeknownst to him) for igniting the writing over and over again by pushing a variety of formal envelopes; Kristjana Gunnars for her writing and her sense of humour; Greg Simison for his writing and his sense of humour; Steven Lattey, Jason Emde, Al Rempel, and Dennis Cooley for being such long-haul correspondents and fellow travellers; Tom Wayman for being my true friend and such an ongoing leader, always showing me the way to live it as well as writing it; Alice Munro (whom I've never met) for being so brilliant and so funny; Glen Sorestad and Sonja Sorestad and Paddy O'Rourke and Al Forrie and Jackie Forrie for creating Thistledown Press and for generously supporting me and my writing so I could keep writing and publishing; Sean Virgo for being the best editor I ever worked with, and one of the most inspiring writers I ever had a chance to talk with; Bev Lent, my sister-in-law, who is such a great reader, and who passes on books to me that I haven't read, like John Williams's *Stoner*; Jay Ruzesky for his writing and his ideas and those wonderful sessions at The Banff Centre and for changing my life with his long and magical friendship; Sharon Thesen for her writing and her knowledge of poetics and her breathtaking and mischievous sense of humour; Mark Nishihara for being my friend and confidante and incredible collaborator; Craig McLuckie for being so damn smart and funny and Scottish and such an inspiring friend through everything we did together as co-conspirators; my wonderful close reader and wizard of literary structure, Mary Ellen Holland for her never-ending support and inspiration; Sean Johnston for his writing and for making me laugh each and every time I see him; Neil Fraser for being such a gifted musician and close friend who I could rant with when things got rough; Jake Kennedy for being such a singularly amazing friend and, in some ways, parallel soul, whose own poetry is off-the-charts astonishing. And finally, the love of my life, the incredible artist whose work graces the cover of this book, my wife Jude Clarke who is a part of everything I have written and whose love I cherish above all else in my world. So there ya go! That might be a wrap.

I also need to thank Wilfrid Laurier University, specifically, Wilfrid Laurier University Press, and even more specifically, Tanis MacDonald and Siobhan McMenemy for approving and encouraging this literary project.

Editor's Note

I'd like to thank (heartily!) Tanis MacDonald for her gracious guidance and for her exceptional eye. And I'm very grateful to Siobhan McMenemy, Murray Tong, and Wilfrid Laurier UP for believing in our project. I'd also like to thank—from the roots—John himself for his friendship, for his astonishing writing and for entrusting me with its stewardship here in this volume. It's just been a total honour and a continual delight to be goin' down this road ... Or, in brief, Yonge Street, John!

lps Books in the Laurier Poetry Series
Published by Wilfrid Laurier University Press

Tim Lilburn	*Desire Never Leaves: The Poetry of Tim Lilburn*, edited by Alison Calder, with an afterword by Tim Lilburn • 2007 • xiv + 50 pp. • ISBN 978-0-88920-514-7
Eli Mandel	*From Room to Room: The Poetry of Eli Mandel*, edited by Peter Webb, with an afterword by Andrew Stubbs • 2011 • xviii + 66 pp. • ISBN 978-1-55458-255-6
Daphne Marlatt	*Rivering: The Poetry of Daphne Marlatt*, edited by Susan Knutson, with an afterword by Daphne Marlatt • 2014 • xxiv + 72 pp. • ISBN 978-1-77112-038-8
Steve McCaffery	*Verse and Worse: Selected and New Poems of Steve McCaffery 1989–2009*, edited by Darren Wershler, with an afterword by Steve McCaffery • 2010 • xiv + 76 pp. • ISBN 978-1-55458-188-7
Don McKay	*Field Marks: The Poetry of Don McKay*, edited by Méira Cook, with an afterword by Don McKay • 2006 • xxvi + 60 pp. • ISBN 978-0-88920-494-2
Duncan Mercredi	*mahikan ka onot: The Poetry of Duncan Mercredi*, edited by Warren Cariou, with an afterword by Duncan Mercredi • 2020 • xx + 82 pp. • ISBN 978-1-77112-474-4
Nduka Otiono	*DisPlace: The Poetry of Nduka Otiono*, selected with an introduction by Peter Midgley and an interview with Nduka Otiono by Chris Dunton • 2021 • xxii + 112 pp. • ISBN 978-1-77112-538-3
Al Purdy	*The More Easily Kept Illusions: The Poetry of Al Purdy*, edited by Robert Budde, with an afterword by Russell Brown • 2006 • xvi + 80 pp. • ISBN 978-0-88920-490-4
Sina Queyras	*Barking & Biting: The Poetry of Sina Queyras*, selected with an introduction by Erin Wunker, with an afterword by Sina Queyras • 2016 • xviii + 70 pp. • ISBN 978-1-77112-216-0
F.R. Scott	*Leaving the Shade of the Middle Ground: The Poetry of F.R. Scott*, edited by Laura Moss, with an afterword by George Elliott Clarke • 2011 • xxiv + 72 pp. • ISBN 978-1-55458-367-6
Sky Dancer Louise Bernice Halfe	*Sôhkêyihta: The Poetry of Sky Dancer Louise Bernice Halfe*, edited by David Gaertner, with an afterword by Sky Dancer Louise Bernice Halfe • 2018 • xx + 96 pp. • ISBN 978-1-77112-349-5
Fred Wah	*The False Laws of Narrative: The Poetry of Fred Wah*, edited by Louis Cabri, with an afterword by Fred Wah • 2009 • xxiv + 78 pp. • ISBN 978-1-55458-046-0

Tom Wayman   *The Order in Which We Do Things: The Poetry of Tom Wayman*, edited by Owen Percy, with an afterword by Tom Wayman • 2014 • xx + 92 pp. • ISBN 978-1-55458-995-1

Rita Wong   *Current, Climate: The Poetry of Rita Wong*, edited by Nicholas Bradley, with an afterword by Rita Wong • 2021 • xxiv + 80 pp. • ISBN 978-1-77112-443-0

Rachel Zolf   *Social Poesis: The Poetry of Rachel Zolf*, selected with an introduction by Heather Milne and an afterword by Rachel Zolf • 2019 • xviii + 80 pp. • ISBN 978-1-77112-411-9

Jan Zwicky   *Chamber Music: The Poetry of Jan Zwicky*, edited by Darren Bifford and Warren Heiti, with a conversation with Jan Zwicky • 2014 • xx + 82 pp. • ISBN 978-1-77112-091-3